Perfect Teens Do (Not) Exist

GBENGA OBAKIN

Perfect Teens Do (Not) Exist

First Published in Great Britain as a softback original in 2019

Edited and designed by Rewrite Agency

Published by Richiefreggs Limited

ISBN: 978-1-9161220-0-0

Email:	info@gbengaobakin.com
	obakinolugbenga@yahoo.com

Website:	www.gbengaobakin.com

Disclaimer

The content of this book is provided for educational and informational purposes only. No responsibility can be taken for any result or outcome from the use of this material.

While every attempt has been made to provide information that is both accurate and effective, the author does not assume any responsibility for the accuracy or use/misuse of this information.

DEDICATION

This book is dedicated to God Almighty and my late father, Michael Olabanji Obakin, who moulded me into the man I am today. May his soul continue to rest in peace. (Amen.)

TABLE OF CONTENTS

ACKNOWLEDGMENTS

Special thanks to God Almighty for how far he has taken me.

I want to say a big thank you to my parents who have played a significant part in pointing me in the right direction. They guided me through life, and I was able to choose my path.

My profound gratitude goes to my big sister, Olaronke who has always been an exemplary leader and a creative critique as well as all my siblings whose support have stood unwavering in all seasons.

My gratitude goes to Tolulope Akinyemi who encouraged me even when there were so many blocks while writing this book.

To everyone who has contributed in one way or the other to this project, thank you very much.

Lastly, I want to say thank you to my better half for believing in me. My wife kept me going and this book would not have been possible without her.

Gbenga Obakin

FORWARD

This book is needed at a time like this: a time where youth crime is escalating at a frightening pace. Almost daily, we hear about knife stabbing and other gang-related activities. An increasing number of young people are not educated, employed or trained due to wrong counsel and influences.

This book will help young people, parents, mentors and other people working with young people to make informed choices. I find the activity section at the end of each chapter practical and thought-provoking.

Experience is the best teacher, and the author has used his expertise to explain some basic life principles especially in making choices and the accompanying consequences. Life is about choices, and decisions always have effects. You are where you are today because of the decisions you took yesterday. Choose wisely!

Ronke Olayemi-Hassan
Operations Director,
Rivers of Joy Initiatives.
Dagenham

INTRODUCTION

The world as I know it has changed.

As children, we were chastised by our mothers and fathers, if we were less than perfect and respectable children. Growing up in Africa meant that you had not just your parents to guide you and provide moral upbringing, but the whole extended family as well. Children were raised by fathers, mother, aunties, grandparents and other members of the extended family. There was no internet at that time except for a black and white TV set that we could only watch if we finished our chores on time. Watching TV was restricted to certain times of the day and beyond the children's control. At that time, there was nothing like social media, and it was a taboo to be seen with harmful substances like drugs or alcoholic drinks.

Travelling abroad was a different ball game entirely. I had to adjust my previous upbringing of how children are raised and look at the British society with a different lens. The world as I knew it in Africa changed again, and I began to see things that, ordinarily, children from where I was coming from would not see.

This above story is not to glamorise Africa or say that there are no unruly children there. On the contrary, our parents used these badly behaved children as examples of who we should not emulate. They told us stories of people who took harmful substances and how they turned out to be a menace to society. They told us to be mindful of peer pressure and do our best to stay away from bad gangs. They told us to read our books so that we could be good citizens in the future. They asked us what we wanted to be in the future and when we said "lawyer, doctor, engineer, banker!" they told us to concentrate on our studies and make them proud.

Today, I want to pass on to you, the lessons I have learnt. It encompasses all that my parents taught me and all that I have gained through the years of experience. No matter your race, gender, sexuality and location, this book contains life lessons that will be beneficial to you in today's world. With the information provided here, you can:

- Boost your self-esteem
- Learn how to be a well-behaved teen

- Improve your reputation

- Say no to peer pressure

- Develop your values

In today's world, it is easy to lose yourself and the things you stand for. As I walk the streets each day, whether in Africa or outside its shores, I see young people with different dreams and aspirations who hope to make something out of their lives. Some are working hard to have good grades, but some might not make it to the finish line because of obstacles like peer pressure, drugs, stealing, etc. that might arise along the way. As youths, wanting a better life shouldn't come at the expense of your morals and personal beliefs.

Perfect Teens Do (Not) Exist is a book written to guide every young person. Think of it as the advice you would get from someone who wishes you well. It is a compass that will come in handy in this fast-changing and technology-driven world. The words of wisdom come from my years of experience in mentoring youths. This book aims to take you by hand through life while providing needed guidance.

I firmly believe that the youths deserve a chance at a good life filled with morals. A young person with a good experience now will have access to a better life in the future. I hope the advice contained therein will help you avoid pitfalls, anticipate bends, interpret road signs and apply the gas pedal where the need arises. There is a whole world of opportunities out there if you can keep your head low and focus on your life.

However, let me make it clear that I do not promise you a bed of roses. Even good youths have different forms of challenges. You need to be ready to take action and be responsible for your actions. Success is hard but achievable. Discipline requires effort and commitment, so you need some level of focus and dedication as you move through life.

At the end of this book, I hope you are inspired to keep good faith. Irrespective of the country where you live, the world needs to feel your best.

All the best,

Gbenga Obakin

1

PEER PRESSURE

*"Confidence is knowing who you are and
not changing it a bit because of
someone's version of reality."*
- Shannon L. Alder

It takes a lot of courage to identify who you are and stick to it. These days, kids face a lot of peer pressure from the media and friends who do all sorts of things to look cool. Don't be afraid to stand out from the crowd and be yourself.

As one who has mentored a lot of young people, I can tell you that living life according to the expectations of others will only make you feel lost and lonely at the end of the day. If you are with a group of friends who force you to do things against your wish, you might want to reconsider that friendship.

There are two types of peer pressure:

- Pressure from external forces that makes you want to fit in
- Pressure from your peers who are pushing you to go further in life.

For example, some friends would prefer that you use the time to study to hang out at some party, drinking, and smoking, while some others know that you need time to study for your GCSE to get admission into college.

If you are getting a lot of peer pressure, you might want to check yourself. Sometimes, we unknowingly attract what we wish. If we do not respect ourselves and have healthy self-esteem, we might be making ourselves open to peer pressure. You need to take care of yourself, have some self-respect and be confident in who you are. Confidence will increase your self-worth in the eyes of your peers and will make them think twice before asking you to do low-level stuff. The more you give in to peer pressure, the more it demands from you. The more you say yes to things that are not cool, the more you lose a part of yourself.

People will either inspire you, be inspired by you or drain you.

One of these options must happen.

A young person is someone who has gotten of age to understand peer pressure and some of its consequences. Simply put, peer pressure is the force from without or the need to fit in so you can be liked or included in your peers' social circle. For teens that are focused, there might be conflict on what to do when peer pressure arises. You might ask, at what point do I say no to peer pressure and still be cool with my friends? It becomes a personal conflict between the mind and body on what one wants to be and what the world wants him or her to be.

The pressure to fit in has turned many teens to misfits who neither know who they are or what they stand for without looking to their friends for permission. They end up unhappy with the company they keep, but at the same time, are unable to stand for their values because of the fear that they will be laughed at and scorned by their friends. Some bright and promising teenagers have taken to blending in, being one with the crowd and never discovering that creating their path is more rewarding than fitting in.

Can Your Parents Trust You with The Right Thing?

It can be tiring for children to listen to the complaints of parents all day. Sometimes, young people want to be left to make the right choices they perceive as right. I get that. But the question is, can your parents trust you to do the right thing? Can they be assured that when you go out with friends, you don't get drunk and get behind the wheel? Can they trust you to stay away from drugs? Can they trust you not to ruin your chance at a scholarship? Can they believe that you will protect yourself from sexually transmitted diseases and seek consent in all you do?

Parents can be overprotective sometimes, and they have no idea that it could be stifling. However, they want the best for you because they love you. They want to be sure that you will make the right choices without having to find out the consequences of your misdeeds if it ever comes to that.

Another reason your parents need to protect you through the manner they have chosen is that they need to provide guidance and control before you become an adult. Nonetheless, the confusion that comes with adolescence has made it difficult for children to talk to their parents about who they are and the adults they want to be. Unapproachable parents can lead many youths to look towards their peers for advice instead of listening to their parents, teachers or mentors. By seeking help from your friends who also need guidance too, you open yourself up to peer pressure.

Finding Nemo

Finding Nemo is one of the highest grossing animated movies of all time from Disney studios. It is an adventure/comedy movie that stars celebrities like Ellen DeGeneres and others. It tells the story of a clownfish that is overly cautious with his son, Nemo who has a foreshortened fin.

His father Marlin constantly reminds Nemo that he's too little to take care of himself. Nemo gives in to peer pressure and undertakes a huge risk which lands him in trouble. His father tries to protect him from danger, but Nemo will stop at nothing to prove himself. His quest to prove himself drives him to be caught by a diver and this leads his father to organize a search for him.

In the process of searching for him with another fish named Dory, they encounter all kinds of complications in a bid to save his son. Nemo, on the other hand, realizes the folly of his actions and does everything possible to return to his father. He learns at the end that his father's caution was not without wisdom. As Marlin searches for his son, he discovers that he was too hard on Nemo and promises to allow Nemo to fight his own battles if he is ever found. When father and son reunite, they discover that both of them are right and every action is done out of love for the other.

What are the moral lessons in this story?

- Overprotective parents can lead their children to embrace peer pressure
- Children will always take risks but, not all risks will have happy endings
- Exploring life is good but be careful as not to be trapped in your exploration
- Peer pressure is surmountable if you are ready to retrace your steps.

If you are continually trying to prove your worth to your friends or do the things they ask you to without question, you will have little time to resist what people throw at you. If you have a group of friends that you are cool with, it should be a group that encourages, motivates and supports you to be the best version of yourself. Who are your friends and what kind of company do you keep? Peer pressure only resorts to a life of pleasing others, being at their beck and call, existing outside who you are, sacrificing your values, living other people's dreams at the expense of your life.

The more you serve as a lap dog to others, the more you lose a piece of yourself. Think of a lap dog. If you throw a fetch at it, it runs to grab it. If you say sit, it will sit. If you say catch, it will catch. If you tell it to stay, it will stay. It is entirely at the beck and call of the owner. In the same way, succumbing to peer pressure means using someone else's standards to measure yours and living by someone else's dictates. Would you rather be your person or an extension of the most beautiful girl in your school? Would you rather have your opinions about events or second everything the most popular boy in your school says? Think about it.

End of Chapter Exercise:

Ask yourself this question and record your honest answer in

the space provided:

Is peer pressure forcing me to fit in when I really shouldn't?

____

____

____

____

Task: Summarize all you have learnt in this chapter

____

____

____

____

To do: What part of yourself do you wish to change?

____

____

____

HOW TO RESIST PEER PRESSURE

At some point, you have to decide to stand your ground and not be easily swayed by other people's opinions.

Mean Girls

Almost every teen has seen the movie, Mean Girls. It is a 2004 teen/comedy movie starring Lindsay Lohan. Its popularity began in the States, before moving on to the U.K, Africa and other parts of the world. Mean Girls follows the story of Cady a home-schooled 16-year-old who ends up falling prey to a group of popular girls known as the Plastics. The group is renowned for its superficial treatment of others. She joins their ranks, and in the process, the influence of Regina, the ring leader of Plastics coaxes Cady into missing her friend's art show and writing bad things about her friends in Regina's burn book. This book is made known to the public, and Cady takes the fall for Regina. Cady loses her worth in the eyes of the friends who knew her before she joined the wrong gang. She loses the trust of her boyfriend, her family and other students who looked up to her. With time, she realised her mistakes and did everything possible to make amends among the aggrieved parties.

What are the lessons we can learn from this story? How can we resist peer pressure or retrace our steps when we make mistakes? Here are some suggestions below:

Have a mind of your own

One of the easiest ways to resist peer pressure is to have a mind of your own. Believe in yourself and know that you have something to offer no matter your circumstances. Don't be a pushover. I understand that we live in a world where we are told what to do- what to wear, what to buy, how to look and things that make us seem cooler to those in our circle. However, having a mind of your own is the first step towards resisting peer pressure. Not only does this reinforce you as a cool person who is kind and will not be a pushover, but people will also come to respect you because you are kind and have a mind of your own.

Have some morals

Personal values or principles are something you should have no matter your age. You are not too young to be seen as a boy or girl of his/her words. Values are important because it keeps you grounded even when a lot of wrongdoings are going on around you. Imbibing strong values like honesty, confidence, respect, integrity, responsibility, etc., helps you live a purposeful life. It also enables you to decide what is right or wrong. Values can be personal, moral, spiritual or cultural. A virtue like integrity makes you a decent person no matter your religious affiliations or your culture. Friendship and tolerance are some of the values you should imbibe as a young adult. The same holds for excellence and forthrightness. Peace, love, respect for one's elders and neighbours, care for human rights, human life and human dignity are some of the universal values people imbibe.

Having values gives you focus. No one wants to associate with someone who has no morals or values. It shows poor upbringing. If one has no discipline or self-control, there would be no zeal to pursue the things that matter in life.

"Drink water and mind your business."

I was surfing the internet a while ago, and I saw this quote: "Drink water and mind your business." I never thought much about it until I looked at it again critically. "Drink water and mind your business" summarizes what a healthy life should be. The quote advocates for healthy living and at the same time urges us to stay away from things that do not concern us. Drinking water will give you a robust immune system while minding your business keeps you preoccupied with your studies and the career you want to have in the future. If you are trying to get into Oxford, Cambridge, Harvard, Yale, Coventry University, Stanford or any college of your choice, you should focus on your studies so you can get in legitimately. You should have little room for anything else.

Health is the greatest gift you can give to yourself. Being healthy requires a sound body and a sound mind. Take good food, eat your vegetables and rest when you can. Ultimately, your parents, most times, know what is best for you. A proper diet will keep your brain sharp, give you the energy to try out new sporting activities and be in good form.

Stay away from toxic people and toxic situations that affect your mental health. It doesn't matter what your childhood is like or if your parents are not the best examples of what you should model your life after. Believe in yourself and the vision you have for the future. If you make the decision today, things can take a U-turn in your life.

Be content with what you have

You cannot be enticed with that which does not excite you. Young people need to be grateful for what they have while trying to work for that which they have not. Your first job might be a store attendant at Waitrose or KFC. It could be washing dishes or helping out by volunteering. Be content with what you have and do not hold grudges with your parents because they can't provide all your needs.

Do away with the spirit of entitlement. Don't steal to satisfy immediate pleasure. If you want something more from life, you need to learn how to work for it like everyone else. Don't be carried away with fast growth. Anything gotten easily is also lost easily. One of the reasons people who are so successful remain successful is that they got whatever success they have through sheer hard work. Nothing is gotten on a platter of gold. Respect people. Respect life and be kind. I cannot over-emphasize this enough.

Who is in your circle?

Growing up in Africa, we have this adage that says "Show me your friends and I will show you who you are." My mother drummed this word of wisdom into my ears, and even when she was not around, I was particular about the company I kept. She made me understand that a good man began with a good boy.

So, I ask you today: who is in your circle? Who are your friends? Do you hang out with the most famous people in your grade because you want to be perceived as cool instead of being with them because they are good friends who will have your interests at heart, the same way you will have theirs? Your friends should motivate you, be your playmates and generally be kind people.

Who are your playmates and what kind of discussions do you have? Do you talk about girls, boys or joints all day? Making good and healthy relationships is important. A healthy relationship is essential and serves as a propelling factor towards greatness. As you go higher in life, good friendships will be there for you through thick and thin.

Take your education seriously

You need to take your school seriously. At this point in your life, education will open a lot of doors for you. Getting into college and excelling at your studies will help make life easier for you. Good grades will give you perfect scores or good enough scores to progress in class as you move from grade to grade. The key is being excellent by studying. Being excellent might come with its share of scholarships and recognition in extra-curricular activities or your studies.

Being excellent however comes with reading, studying and learning as much as you can. It will involve improving yourself daily. It begins with a basic education in school, listening to your parents and teachers. This also means furthering your education, having a specialty and improving your craft. Give yourself something to aim for continuously and be motivated irrespective of the present challenges. Develop your values. Goodness and kindness never go out of fashion.

End of Chapter Exercise:

Do I possess any of the values mentioned above? If yes, what are they? If no, how can I cultivate them?

____

____

____

____

Task: Summarize all you have learnt in this chapter

____

____

____

____

To do: What part of yourself do you wish to change?

____

____

____

3

FINDING YOUR PURPOSE

As a teenager finding your footing in today's world, you need to pay attention to your inner voice. To find happiness, we must look inwards. True happiness comes from being comfortable in our skin, being true to ourselves, living our dreams and being proud of what makes us unique.

Perhaps, it is easier said than done. However, the trick is to ask yourself several questions:

- What makes life worth living?

- What is my purpose in life?

- Am I living my best experience yet?

- How would I like to be remembered?

- What do I admire about others?

- What makes me unique?

It will also help if you reflect on your unique personalities and how you always picture your life. Knowing the things you hold dear can also be the missing link you may need to make that move towards self-discovery.

It is understandable if you are at a crossroad especially when it comes to purpose. After all, you might say that you have your whole life ahead of you. If you are between the ages of twelve to eighteen, this talk about purpose will be beneficial to you.

Here's why you need to define your purpose from an early age: It gives you a sense of direction. It makes you grounded even without your parents' rules at home. If you take time to define who you want to be in the future, you can start now towards planning the man or woman you want to be.

What do you want to be in the future? An engineer? A pilot? A builder? A lawyer? A writer? An artist? A plumber? The Prime minister of England? Each of these occupations come with some level of responsibility. Those who plan to go into politics start from an early age to develop values that are fitting for the job. They stay away from scandals, learn the virtues of listening, kindness and apply it to their friends, foes, and neighbours. I am not saying you should be kind just because you want to be a politician. That would be living a false life. My point is that learning these virtues should become second nature to you now so that you can grow up to be the man or woman that you can be- which is the best version of yourself. Whatever it is you are gifted in, ensure you are successful and excel in it. For some, academics might not be it, but even if you are an entrepreneur, be focused and put in your best.

Take a moment to highlight your belief system and values like honesty, kindness, perseverance, etc. and seek out like-minded friends who have the same values as you. If you have a friend that is always talking about sex, parties, girls, and boys without facing his or her studies, you might want to rearrange your priorities and move with people of like minds. People of similar minds should not be confused with the crowd. While the latter can range from anyone who doesn't share your values to a group of fair-weather friends, people with like minds may include mentors, teachers and those who encourage you to be more. These are people you feel at ease with, and they also help you grow and flourish per your set goals.

While it is true that people are different and that following the crowd or fitting in isn't necessarily wrong, everyone has individual goals and aspirations. Right or wrong depends on inner conviction, no matter the differences. Discovering your path means being comfortable in your skin. It means we do not compare our lives with anyone as we have found our true nature and we live according to its dictates.

In life, there will always be someone who is more beautiful, stronger, and more talented. In the same vein, there will be people who you are better than. So instead of trying to live a life of another individual, it is best to chart your course early on in life and keep at it instead of being distracted by those whose beliefs do not align with yours. Do not force your friendship on anyone. Fulfilling your best potential to the best of your ability should be the goal and rather than being others, try to be you.

Life makes so much sense when there is diversity. It wouldn't be any fun if we were all trying to be the same. Your rightful place in the world is essential. ***You (insert your name here) are important.*** Let go of who you think you should be and be who you were meant to be. Don't change so people can like you. Be yourself, and the right people will love you as you are. Finding your purpose is something you have to do for yourself.

I remember this incident because it is still fresh in my memory like it was yesterday. In high school, I had a lot of friends, but over time, I had to sit down to choose who I wanted to be friends with. If I were to categorize the impact of these friends in my life, I would group them into two:

- The ones that got me in trouble during school time and with my parents
- The ones who contributed positively to my life especially academically

I decided to steer clear of the former, and that single decision is the foundation of who I am today. Those friends I chose to be with continued to inspire me up till date and I can tell you every single one of them has done well for himself.

It is necessary for youths at a certain age to start having a vision of what they want for themselves in the future. The kind of friends we have and hang out with will be a significant determinant of whether that vision will be achieved or not. I know there is a lot of peer pressure especially at this age, but one needs to identify and establish what works for him/her regardless.

I was not always a good boy. You can say that I decided to be focused "under duress." One of the things that made me decide to straighten my path was the fact that my parents and my teachers had begun to complain about some of the behaviours I was exhibiting. I started arguing a lot to justify what I was getting wrong and those things they were complaining about.

At home, I was not studying as much as I was expected to. I

neglected chores (thank God my African mother knew this was just a phase or else, I would have received the 'stick' on my head on many occasions) and distanced myself from my parents because I thought they were old school people with old school ideas. However, all that changed when I took a step back to evaluate my life and transform hitherto cooperative arrangements.

It is never too early to start developing good habits. Persistence and constant personal progression are some of the most important things when it comes to accomplishing goals. It is better to form the bedrock of one's future at an early age.

Enough with the Motivation, I Want to Live My Life!

'It's my life. I can do whatever I want with it. You only live once.'

Have you made that statement before? Does it sound familiar? I'll bet it does! I said it so many times while growing up and so, I know you might have said it at least once.

If we are honest, I must let you know that no parent expects a perfect teen. **Perfect teens do (not) exist!** They know that you will make mistakes and they are ready to comfort you when the tears have stopped.

A lot of parents have heard these words before: "It's my life! You can't tell me how to live it!" They probably said the same thing to their parents while growing up. However, as much as I am trying not to be a spoil-sport, I must let you know that the idea of freedom can have a positive or negative impact on you depending on how you utilize the liberty. In the UK, the legal age is sixteen years old. In other parts of the world, the age of consent ranges from seventeen to twenty-one. The legal age in this context is the age where you can move out of your parents' house, buy your drink and vote. Nonetheless, this is the age one needs to exercise a lot of caution because this stage can form the bedrock of one's future. Some people make mistakes at this stage, and it haunts them forever. Some make mistakes and have a chance to mend it in the future. The question is, are you willing to take that chance?

Let me tell you another story. While I was in college, I had a friend that had to lie to his parents about going somewhere else but travelled about 200 miles for a party with his friends. Due to recklessness, they got drunk and used different dangerous drugs. They were involved in a ghastly motor accident in which he died instantly. His parents found out on the news. There was no chance for him to correct his mistakes, although some survivors of the crash recovered enough to mull over their behaviour and turn a new leaf.

From my own experience of handling freedom, I'll give you another peek into my life. I started clubbing, partying, drinking and smoking. I forgot all about my studies, and in a particular year, I did thirteen courses but failed nine out of the thirteen. That year, I remember sitting down and ruminating over my life. I asked myself what I wanted to live for and how I would achieve this. My grades were terrible, and I had to make a quick decision to either concentrate on my life or drop out and become useless. Right there and then, I redefined my life, developed focus and dropped some of those habits that were going to destroy my future. I eventually came out with a good grade, but I can tell you vividly that some of my mates never got it back together up till today.

Purpose is vital because it gives you a clear picture of where you ought to be. Passion is also important. It is easier to pursue a career or livelihood through one's passion. Moreover, education plays a significant role in shaping the youth's future. Therefore, education should not be at the detriment of passion. One should marry the two together. You never know where either will land you in life.

End of Chapter Exercise:

Would you rather a clean life and no future guilt or a life where you always have to look over your shoulder?

____

____

____

____

Task: Summarize all you have learnt in this chapter

____

____

____

____

To do: What part of yourself do you wish to change?

____

____

____

____

4

DRUGS, ALCOHOL, AND ADDICTION

Not everyone can speak to young people about drugs, alcohol, and addiction without condemning them. I am not here to preach. I am neither a preacher nor a religious fanatic. Here's what I'll tell you for free: when anything is not done in moderation, it always has adverse consequences.

Excessive use of drugs, over-imbibing alcohol, porn addiction, and other addictions are some of the things that plague young people today. It is a problem that needs urgent solutions. In this age of social media, things are amplified for the gram, and almost every teen wants to show off some bottles or cigarettes for the gram. Why? They think it makes them look cool!

I'll tell you why you should stay away from this kind of lifestyle without mincing words: those who take to smoking joints frequently or engaging in addictive activities never end up victorious if they continue with this bad habit. Your parents, teachers, and mentors want the best for you. They want to be associated with someone who makes the news for good stuff. They want to be called to a parent-teacher meeting with tales of how wonderful their child is. They want to be proud of their child and look towards a healthy and progressive future for them.

There is no win-win situation with drug and alcohol addiction. People who start sniffing begin with 'harmless little puffs,' and before you know it, it becomes a full-blown addiction. It is never the plan to get addicted. It happens unexpectedly; hence, the reason it is dangerous. Not only does it cloud your memory, but it is also an expensive habit that clouds your judgment. Smoking joints might start as fun, but after a while, you are drawn in before you know it. The ripple effects are far-reaching! Besides, drugs are so expensive that with your level of income, you probably can't keep up unless you resort to stealing or doing all sorts of illegal things. It is just not worth the stress.

Many youths try out alcohol, tobacco, or drugs before they get to the age of sixteen. For some, it is pornography and indiscriminate sex with everything that breathes. Some try these substances a few times and stop. Others who aren't so lucky keep at it until it becomes a full-fledged monster eating deep into their lives.

This is not a scary drug and alcohol talk. In my days, I took a couple of drinks and partied hard. However, I knew when to draw the line because my mother's words would always ring in my ears. I had two options, basically: allow these substances to control me or have a good life and indulge when I am in full control of my faculties as a mature adult. I chose the latter which is why you are reading this book today.

I am here to present the facts and hope that you make the right choice. Some have lost loved ones to drugs; lost homes, dignity and a few ribs to an alcoholic father or substance-abusive mother.

Once drugs, porn or alcohol has you in its clutches, it impedes the workings of the brain, and because of this, stopping drug or alcohol use is not by sheer will. Bad things are irresistible! Humans can't help but experiment. People try new things all the time because it seems exciting or cures boredom for a while. It takes discipline to see what is wrong and say, 'Not today!'

Let me tell you about John. He was a young kid whose friends thought he was weak because he didn't drink and smoke. They made fun of him, and it hurt. He had to join them to show he was not weak. He drank and drank and in the process, lost the same friends who pushed him into it. He became violent and hit his siblings coupled with the fact that he had to steal to feed his addiction. John was diagnosed with lung cancer at 19. He died within three months.

Peer pressure also plays a role in fueling addictions. People think a cigarette hanging by the side of their mouth makes them look cool. They want to be seen as the most current kid on the block. They believe taking drugs, smoking and taking alcohol makes them feel grown. I often wonder why people smoke when it is stated clearly on the packet that "Smoking kills!" People die from smoke-related incidents every year, yet the cigarette is one of the highest selling commodities! The contradiction baffles me I must say.

Quick exercise: What's your current addiction? Can you recall the reason you got addicted in the first place?

Did you know?

> *Alcohol and drugs are the leading causes of crime and suicide among youths.*

More than 23 million people over the age of 12 are addicted to alcohol and other drugs, affecting millions of people…spouses, children, family members, friends, colleagues, and neighbours.

Marijuana and Grades: 19.3% of students aged 12-17 who receive average grades of "D" or lower used marijuana in the past month and 6.9% of students with grades of "C" or above used marijuana in the past month.

Source: NIDA/NCADD

The signs and symptoms of drug and alcohol addiction, as well as the short and long-term effects of alcohol abuse, don't always occur in isolation. Some youths go as far as combining drugs and alcohol to increase their level of intoxication.

Studies have shown that the reason students indulge in things they know is terrible for them lies in the following:

- Trying to seek approval from a group
- Low sense of self-worth
- Lack of daily planning and set goals
- The need to drown sorrows

Many A-level students are at risk of developing a drug and alcohol addiction due to peer pressure or trying to seek approval from a group they are associated with. They want to be seen as a champion among their friends, so they will do anything to feel among. Friends shape us in more ways than we realize and it is crucial you differentiate between friends you hang out with and regular acquaintances you see in school.

Show me your friends, and I will show you who you are! Everyone fears rejection. Some people would rather break the law, disobey their parents and even risk their own lives just to be accepted by their peers. Students have done stupid things to impress their friends. Scores of teenagers all across the country are doing things they don't want to in a bid to fit in.

Here's food for thought: our friends don't live with the consequences of our decisions; we do. I hope that with the knowledge you will get from this book, you will re-consider seeking validation from any group you belong to.

Have confidence in yourself and your abilities so as not to fall prey to those who sweet-talk you into doing drugs. Drugs and alcohol will only give you a reprieve and a false sense of bravado.

Young adults are in prison because of drug and alcohol-related crimes, and many of them are slowly undergoing rehabilitation. I think that avoiding the whole experience would have been the best choice. Once the drugs wear off, you are back to the ground. Drugs and alcohol make you regularly do illegal things, disappoint your family, or not live up to the person you know you could be. If you are struggling with your self-esteem— if you don't like who you are, the best way to feel good about yourself is by making choices that you're proud of.

Be productive

The idle mind is the devil's workshop. Make good use of your time and be productive. Have a plan. When you fail to plan, you plan to fail. When you have so much free time on your hands without any form of productive output, something is bound to occupy your mind. Boredom leads to experimenting and most times, people turn to substance abuse to relieve boredom. People who get bored easily are those with a lot of unproductive time on their hands. A lot of trouble happens when there is no sense of daily or monthly direction. The sense of direction and daily planning will leave you too busy to think of something not worth your while.

Set daily, monthly or yearly goals. Abide by it. Try to chip off what you have achieved off the block. Get a hobby. Plan ahead. Occupy yourself with your favourite interests. Break away from the routine. Find something fun to do. Fill your life with productive thoughts and activities and try new things.

Sometimes students get into fights with their parents or at

school, and this can lead them to get expelled. For some, things might be tough at the moment. Students use alcohol and drugs to numb the pain, and I get it. However, I know it will not help. It just distracts from the real issues and makes everything worse. Do not use drugs as a way to escape the pain. Get help.

The visible signs of addiction include:

- Blurry vision, hallucinations and, red eyes.
- Being overly tired
- Trying to escape school, drop in grades, skipping classes and uncoordinated talk.
- Less interest in bonding and little interest in school activities
- Needle marks on arms or other parts of the body.
- The stench of alcohol on clothes or books

Quick Exercise: Do I recognize any of these signs in myself?

Drugs and alcohol affect your health and can give you liver damage, asthma, lung cancer or blood poisoning. Drunken people can also get hurt and cause accidents. Emergency rooms in hospitals get packed out every weekend because of drunk injuries. People get involved in fights; people are in car accidents, and a whole lot of people make rash and illogical decisions. As for cigarettes, scientists say that your brain is fully developed when you reach the age of twenty-five so by inhaling weed you're not giving your mind a chance to develop fully. That's a huge regret to live with just for a quick fix. Drunks take rash actions. It has to do with the hormone triggered at the point of intoxication. A lot of smokers end up with regret because they get sick. These sicknesses cost a lot to treat. One who smokes regularly spends thousands of pounds and is far more likely to develop a mental illness such as depression and anxiety disorder including paranoia or anxiety attacks.

One wrong decision made in a moment of weakness can change the rest of your life. Don't let it be your last. Every year there are thousands of people killed due to drunk driving. Try not to join the statistics. Studies have shown that some of these drugs contain heaps of crazy substances like flea powder, rat poison, bleach and cleaning items. Is that what you want to inhale?

The world has lost far too many bright stars to drug addiction and alcohol abuse. From Whitney Houston and Amy Winehouse to Cory Monteith and Philip Seymour Hoffman; celebrity deaths from drug and alcohol overdoses leave millions of fans in mourning. Could these stars have been saved? Maybe.

Amy Winehouse

Let me tell you about Amy Winehouse. Amy Jade Winehouse was an English singer-songwriter. She was known for her deep vocals and eclectic mix of musical genres including soul, jazz and Rand B (Gazette Review). She was one of the most versatile artists in the world. She was a success in the U.K and had five Grammy awards to her name within the short while she was in the industry. She was the first British woman to win five Grammys.

She died in 2011 due to alcohol poisoning. She was also known to rely on a lot of drugs. Winehouse's public image of critical and commercial success versus personal turmoil prompted media comment. The *New Statesman* called Amy 'a filthy-mouthed down-to-earth diva' while *Newsweek* called her 'a perfect storm of sex kitten, raw talent and poor impulse control.' In 2008, her drug problems threatened her career. On so many occasions, her record label wanted to let her go due to her issues. She had a long history with substance abuse, and it was a problem that reared its head every time. She was prevented from travelling and performing at the Grammy Awards ceremony in the US due to failing a drug test. (Wikipedia)

Three days before her death, Amy's bodyguard found her intoxicated, and in subsequent days, she drank some more. She was pronounced dead in the morning after drinking all night and into the wee hours of the morning. Forensic experts found two bottles of vodka in her room. Her blood and alcohol content was five times the legal drink-drive limit. This led to her sudden death.

It doesn't matter how many stories I have shared. For some, their opinion on using drugs or drinking alcohol will remain the same. I hope it will not be too late. Maybe because the TV shows it's cool or perhaps they believe "it will never happen to me". Some people believe that they are exceptions to the rule. They think that they will never get caught by their parents or their school or that they won't be the person who has the misfortune. They believe this idea that even though it could happen; it would not happen to them. Do you want to take chances?

One thing I am sure of is that if you keep abusing substance, you will get addicted. It is as sure as rain. There are no exceptions. There is no big star and non-celebrity status when it comes to imbibing. Something always happens. The question is, when? If you or someone you know is struggling with addiction –don't fight alone. Talk to someone or get help. Don't be a statistic.

Seek Help If You Suffer From Substance Abuse

Reaching out to help someone with an alcohol or drug problem is not easy. Although the signs are always there, it might be hard for addicts to admit that they have a problem. If it is you, seek help. If it is your friend, don't be afraid to recommend that they see a therapist. Most addicts do not admit it even to themselves. All too often, close friends and family turn a blind eye to the situation hoping that the person will eventually see reason to quit those bad attitudes and addictions. However, addiction will not go away if unattended to. More denial prevents the person from appreciating the full extent of the problem and its consequences. Heavy drinkers are less able to make conscious choices about their drinking, and so the involvement of family, friends, and employers can make a difference.

This might be one of the hardest decisions to make, but I assure you that it will be one of the best decisions. You owe it to yourself to seek help from whatever ails you.

Parents, to help a student with addiction, be non-confrontational and persuasive. Don't be judgmental. Avoid embarrassing confrontations. Show that you are there to help. Talk to them and explain the consequences addiction can have in their lives in the long run. Showcase the facts about their drinking or drug abuse without mincing words. Try to avoid being all righteous or demanding. Make them understand that they have an illness that should be taken care of before it eats deep into their system and causes irreparable damages. A healthier alternative which may serve as a leveraging tool might come in handy. Joining a support group has its advantages. This way, your child sees that he or she is not alone and that there are a lot of people willing to embark on this journey towards wellness with them.

As with any illness, drug and alcohol addiction respond best to early intervention.

End of Chapter Exercise:

Do you need help with an addiction? Write it down

____

____

____

____

Task: Summarize all you have learnt in this chapter

____

____

____

To do: What part of yourself do you wish to change?

____

____

____

GOOD INTERNET AND THE RIGHT ATTITUDE

In this age of technological advancement and social media, there is a lot of dark web on the internet. Everywhere we turn on the internet; there is a video, page or directive that is the antithesis of moral upbringing. Despite the safety measures and age restrictions put in place, the internet is still a deep abyss that if not monitored, can lead you astray. As a young person, what are you watching?

Technological boom cannot be stopped- after all- the future is now, but as a teen that has a vision and destination, you need to be selective of the information you consume. You need to take responsibility and protect your space from distractions.

The internet is a double-edged sword. On the one hand, the

internet is a vast land where people can be educated about any topic they choose. On the other, it is a deep gorge, a platform used by people to do deep dark things while hiding behind screens. Know which path you are taking and do not get lost. Use the internet for good.

Developing the Right Attitude

Attitude is everything. It is the core of what humans are. Your attitude will either attract or chase people away from you. A lot of talented young individuals will go far if they develop the right attitude towards life. I have seen kids with talents and ideas and big dreams of how they envisage their future, but sadly, their bad attitude might stop them from achieving their goals if they do not change.

Do away with entitlement. No one owes you anything. The world is not fair, and ideally, you are only entitled to what you work for. Although some may come from privileged backgrounds and this may give them a head start in life, it doesn't guarantee a bright future ahead.

Here are six tips you need to be an almost perfect youth.

1. Maintain the right mindset

Everything you want to possess begins in the mind. Without

the right mindset towards situations and the right attitude towards life, you might not have headway in life. Pay attention to what you listen to and what you think. The mind is one of the powerful tools you need to turn dreams into reality. One of the reasons so many young people are stuck today is because they feed their minds with negative thoughts. They listen to everything and anything and are easily distracted by what they see on social media. They are carried away with the life on the gram and will stop at nothing to replicate what they are feeding their minds with.

2. Don't underestimate your talent

Remove every self-doubt you might have about your inadequacies. Don't think too little of yourself and your talent. You are capable of achieving what you set your mind to. Negative influences can only cut short your potential if you let it. I have seen a lot of young people lose confidence in themselves, procrastinate their goals, settle for less, mingle with the wrong crowd or resign themselves to fate.

You owe it to yourself to take charge of your life. There will always be things looking for your attention out there, but only you can decide what you want to pay attention to. You are the master of your mind, and you are responsible for the kind of thoughts you nurture in your mind. Read as much as you can.

Learn as much as you can. Ignore the present circumstances and focus on what is ahead of you. Say no to a life of mediocrity and refuse to take what life throws at you with folded hands. Be an active participant in your life. Step out of your comfort zone and dare the impossible.

3. Live an honest and modest life

As a straightforward child, man or woman is one who lives by the truth and is ready to face the consequences of living by the truth. Honesty and modesty are some of the most admired traits in successful individuals. To create a good and worthy life, honesty is a trait you should be known for.

As a child growing up in Africa, my parents taught me the importance of honesty. Back then, a good name was synonymous with riches. It was not improper to see families who had nothing and could boast of nothing except their family name. They were content with what they had and lived within their means.

Those values followed me wherever I went, and now that I live in the UK, I have come to appreciate the importance of honesty. It has shaped my dealings as a man and has endeared me to people I interact with. Honesty and modesty weren't what I learnt in my old age. It was the values I imbibed when

I was much younger- especially during my teenage years- that I have maintained to date. Somewhere along the line, your honesty will be tested. Come what may stay true to your values.

Telling lies can be exhausting. Let's say you want to go to Stacy's party without letting your parents know. You have to prepare a lie to get yourself out of the house, prepare another lie for why you smell like you fell into a barrel of wine and another lie for when you will get back home. That is if the cops do not catch you driving and drinking or you do not have an accident due to drunk driving. The lies are numerous, and it will take time to memorize all the lies. Telling lies are hard.

4. Take advantage of all opportunities available to you

There are a lot of opportunities available to you in form of scholarships, internships, and volunteer opportunities. Getting into these programs will require truthfulness on your part and some level of exemplary behaviour. Not many programs want to identify with unruly youths or people with notorious character. The more sterling your character is, the more chances you have making it into programs. Some of these opportunities require recommendation letters from your teachers and the principals of your school. No one would be willing to write you a recommendation letter if you will jeopardize their reputation or bring them shame and disgrace. Applying for opportunities- jobs, scholarships, boot camps, teen leadership training- outside your country will require some background check including social media activities. If anything negative turns up on their radar, you might be deprived of your shot at an endless world of possibilities.

Lasting success is created by a strong character inspired by the right value-adding system. Once you learn to overcome fear, you will realize your full potential. Fear prevents a lot of young people from reaching for the stars. Some of these fears include fear of failure, fear of what people will say, fear of rejection, fear of not being good enough and many other concerns that are in their minds. Understand today that fear is a natural element that comes with growth. Fear is to be expected especially if what you are attempting to do has not been done before. Being afraid is not a sign of weakness; rather it shows that you are human. Being scared should never be the problem; what you do with fear is the most important thing.

5. Don't deny your flaws

Everyone has flaws; some people's weaknesses are more pronounced than the others. Flaws are what make us human. It is part of life's journey. Embrace these flaws for what they are and do everything possible to ensure they are properly managed. Managing your flaws involves taking actions despite your shortcomings and weaknesses. It involves adjusting your mental, emotional and physical state to embrace all life has in store for you. It involves being the best version of yourself and trying to be better than you were yesterday.

6. Take rejections in stride

Rejections hurt. Whether it's the girl that refused to accept your prom date or the boy that refused to read the love letters tucked in between his books. No one likes to be rejected and that's a perfectly normal reaction. Life has been structured in such a way that each person gets the highs and the lows. One morning you have the perfect scores on your SATs, and the next day, your school team doesn't make it to the championships. When life tries to show its hand, how well you handle it is the difference between success and failure. Don't give up on life because a few things are not going in your favour. A lot more things will not go in your favour, and that's perfectly fine. Remain optimistic and keep moving. Even if that email is not the response you were expecting, shut the system and move on with life. Tomorrow is pregnant. Celebrate the little wins you have in your life and look forward to many more.

Develop the habit of gratitude- for little things and big things.

Don't wait till you accomplish big goals before you pat yourself at the back. Develop a winning attitude, remain self-motivated, remain happy, be happy with your company, build your confidence and start achieving.

I wish you all the best in life!

End of Chapter Exercise:

Write down the things you need to develop the right attitude

____

____

____

____

Task: Summarize all you have learnt in this chapter

____

____

____

____

To do: What part of yourself do you wish to change?

____

____

____

____

ABOUT THE AUTHOR

Olugbenga Obakin is a financial-crime consultant based in the United Kingdom. He had his first degree in Geology from the prestigious premier university in Nigeria, University of Ibadan. He worked in different banks in Nigeria before proceeding to the United Kingdom to bag a Masters in Business Administration from Sheffield Hallam University, Sheffield.

Olugbenga is involved in youth mentoring and coaching. He is passionate about helping youths make good choices early in life. His passion, no doubt, has come from his background, having strict parents, his quest to explore life as a teenager, the choices he made, the choices made by others around him and the consequences thereafter. He believes in the saying "experience is the best teacher". He has a good relationship with youths while mentoring them because he has seen it all and was able to make his choices through all these to become who he is today.

Olugbenga is involved with Rivers of Joy Initiatives, a non-profit organisation based in Essex through which he reaches out to youths during programmes and activities. He is also involved in catering for the homeless by providing food to sheltered homes. Olugbenga also features in open mic events and slams as well as spoken word events in the Northeast, England.

His greatest passion is to impact society through the youths as the youths are the future of tomorrow. He is happily married.

AUTHOR'S NOTE

I once read a citation which says "we all have the power to make choices in life, but we do not have the power to choose the consequences that come with it". This has inspired me a lot over time.

If you are reading this, I want to believe you have found time to read this book and I appreciate the time you have invested in reading it. I hope you have found it very educative and it will encourage you to make good choices in life. Kindly share the book and the contents therein with family and friends. Let's keep spreading the news of choices and consequences.

Thank you